BOLD KIDS

Helicopters

**EDUCATIONAL FACTS
CHILDREN'S AVIATION BOOK**

No part of this book may be reproduced or used in any way or form or by any means whether electronic or mechanical, this means that you cannot record or photocopy any material ideas or tips that are provided in this book.
Copyright 2022

All images in this book have been reproduced with the knowledge and prior consent of the artists concerned, and no responsibility is accepted by producer, publisher, or printer for any infringement of copyright or otherwise, arising from the contents of this publication.

Helicopters are flying machines that can land on aircraft carriers or in remote areas.

The ability to fly forward, backward, sideways, and in tight spaces makes these aircraft very versatile. In one famous test, H. Ross Perot Jr. and J.W. Coburn, both former presidential candidates, took 29 days to circle the earth.

FLIGHT CHARACTERISTICS

Helicopters are air vehicles that fly through the air using the thrust created by rotating rotors. This gives helicopters the ability to perform maneuvers that airplanes cannot.

They also have the ability to do vertical take-off and landing. A helicopter's cruising speed is much lower than that of an airplane, which is due to the complexity of the aircraft's flight control systems.

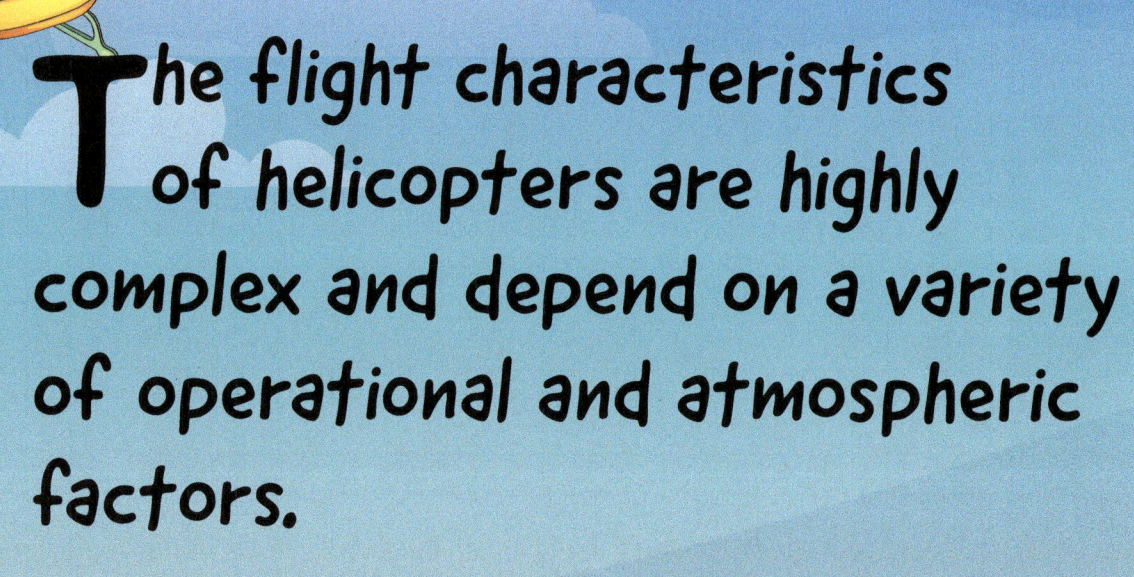

The flight characteristics of helicopters are highly complex and depend on a variety of operational and atmospheric factors.

To determine these variables at random would require extensive flight time, which would be very expensive. As such, helicopter flight tests focus on takeoff and landing characteristics and on rational piloting techniques.

CAPABILITIES

The modern helicopter is a versatile machine that has several distinct functions. Some are designed to carry passengers, while others are used to transport cargo.

Modern helicopters have a variety of capabilities, and the next generation will be much more capable than the current generation. During the 1960s, the YH-16B and XHCH-1 were the standard cargo helicopters. They had a capacity of around 22,000 pounds and could hover at a height of 5,600 feet.

Helicopters have become an integral part of the military, enabling ground forces to provide air mobility. Their low flying profile means they can be used in a variety of missions and environments.

The capability to hover over an area reduces reaction time and allows them to be integrated with other assets. This allows for extended reach and better coverage for ground-based forces.

FAMOUS PILOTS

It's hard to believe, but famous helicopter pilots are a real thing. They rescue the most unfortunate people in the sky, and they often fly in dangerous conditions.

These heroes have a unique perspective on aviation safety and regulations. They often share their experiences with the public to inspire others. The following are just a few of these illustrious men and women.

Bahnsen earned the Distinguished Flying Cross for his extraordinary efforts in the war in Vietnam. In one particularly memorable incident, he made a direct pass on enemy forces attacking U.S. ground forces, and he landed in front of enemy elements.

He then led troops forward and destroyed enemy positions, earning him his second Distinguished Flying Cross. The following month, he received a third Distinguished Flying Cross.

COST

Helicopters are an expensive investment, so if you want to buy one, you should know how much they cost. The price of a new helicopter varies depending on its capacity and design.

Larger models are typically more expensive than smaller ones. Other factors to consider include the size and number of seats. The size of the helicopter also affects the costs of its maintenance and insurance.

The cost of acquiring a helicopter is higher than for a fixed-wing aircraft, but this cost goes down as the number of hours it is used increases. Another cost that you need to consider is hangar rental, which is required regardless of flight hours, but benefits from economies of scale.

For example, it costs less to rent a hangar for 65 hours of operation than to rent a hangar for 200 hours. Additionally, helicopter training and maintenance costs are higher than for a fixed-wing aircraft.

Milton Keynes UK
Ingram Content Group UK Ltd.
UKHW050347130923
428539UK00008B/83